It Could Have Gone Another Way

It Could Have Gone Another Way

Poems by

Lynda La Rocca

© 2024 Lynda La Rocca. All rights reserved.
This material may not be reproduced in any form, published,
reprinted, recorded, performed, broadcast,
rewritten, or redistributed without
the explicit permission of Lynda La Rocca.
All such actions are strictly prohibited by law.

Cover design by Shay Culligan
Cover photo by Stephen M. Voynick, State Highway 82 between
Twin Lakes and Independence Pass, Colorado
Author photo by Stephen M. Voynick

ISBN: 978-1-63980-642-3

Kelsay Books
502 South 1040 East, A-119
American Fork, Utah 84003
Kelsaybooks.com

To Dante, who remembers.

And to dearest Steve, forever.

"We always may be what we might have been."
—Adelaide Anne Procter, from *A Legend of Provence*

Acknowledgments

The poems listed below originally appeared in the following venues, occasionally in slightly altered versions and always with my gratitude:

Blue Mountain Arts, 34th Biannual Poetry Contest (online only): "My Cousin Angela Keeps It Safe"
Chaparral Poetry Forum: "High School English Teacher," "Seeing the Future/My Father's Eyes"
Encore, Prize Poems of the National Federation of State Poetry Societies, Inc.: "This Is Only a Test (October 1962)," "Thinking About Screaming"
SageGreenJournal (online only): "Home Is Where You Hang Your Hat"
The Stillness Between: "Runs with Scissors"
Upon Waking: 58 Voices Speaking Out From the Shadow of Abuse: "Declaration" (reprinted in *Columbine at 45: Keeping Poetry Alive!*)

Contents

Declaration	11
Kill Joy	12
Mother's Day, a Memory	13
Going for Ice Cream	14
This Is Only a Test (October 1962)	17
Runs with Scissors	19
Dunk	20
Family Barbecue	22
Grandpa's Weeds	24
In the Trenches	25
See You Later, Alligator	27
Infant of Prague	29
September, Starting High School	32
Mr. Levine Teaches the Goy About Passover	35
Another Day	38
O Holy Night	39
High School English Teacher	40
Marriage Material: According to My Father	41
Momma	42
Like Foxfire	44
My Cousin Angela Keeps It Safe	45
Seeing the Future/My Father's Eyes	46
Here We Go Again	47
Thinking About Screaming	48
All There Is	49
Joker Is Wild	50
Love as Theory	51
After Life	53
Home Is Where You Hang Your Hat	54
It Could Have Gone Another Way	56

Declaration

This is how
I refuse
to be what
you require.

No, I say.
Lies, I say.
Stop, I say.
Don't.
If there is a hell, I say,
then
you will go there.
You'll go there,
I'll pray for you,
you won't deserve it.

But praying is how I stay
angry at God.
And this is how,
now
when it's dark,
I can sleep.

Kill Joy

after Kay Ryan

It isn't easy
to kill joy.

It takes
hard work
and planning

to erase
another's grin
and poke
a pin into
the shining eye.

It is a talent
polished, honed by
deft determination

that even then
cannot keep out the light.

Mother's Day, a Memory

I want the gladiolus, of all
the flowers in the shop, the
spiky, showy, prettiest, the
fireworks of color—orange,
pink, red, yellow, one is white.
And I choose seven stalks for
you, and Daddy gives the lady
coins and dollars, and she wraps
the gladiolus in green tissue, puts
them in a long, gold box, and I
can't wait to give them to you,
I'm so happy, I'm so proud, I
know you'll be so happy, too.
And we drive home, I'm
holding out the box, and Daddy
lights a cigarette, you're shouting,
"Why'd you let her go and buy
those funeral flowers?" and
the box, the blossoms broken,
skids across the kitchen floor.

Going for Ice Cream

My father's always coffee—
in Little Italy,
the Bronx,
Atlantic City boardwalk—
no matter where we'd drive,
he'd find a shop or ice-cream stand
and buy a cone of coffee.

"Whaddaya mean, you don't like coffee?"
he'd yell,
my baby tongue still sticking to
his frozen, carpet-colored cream.

"I just don't like it,"
quietly I'd answer,
handing back the cone
he'd always make me taste,
wondering (but silently)
why anyone would want to eat
great gobs of icy coffee—
hot and liquid, it was bad enough,
so bitter,
back before I'd grown
into six cups a day.

My little brother's butter pecan
dripping on fake leather
in the back of the Impala,
Dad's reward, company car,
for selling big.

"Ahhh, whadda you know?"
my father's eyes would find me
in the rearview mirror
and he'd wink.
"Watch what the hell you're doing,"
he would holler at my brother
as my brother's eyes grew heavy.
"Clean that up for him—
he's ruining the seat."

Then he'd reach back—
"Lemme taste that,"
and he'd snag my maple walnut—
that's the one I always asked for—
and he'd crunch the last bite of his cone
and get to work on mine.
"How the hell can you eat this?"
he'd ask and grin,
then grab my brother's cone
and lick the melting butter cream
and break a big pecan between his teeth.

"Mom, which one's your favorite?"
I would ask, hanging sticky hands
over the back of her powder-blue passenger seat,
wanting to touch her perfect hair.
"Oh, I don't know," she'd say
and not look back.

"Whaddaya mean, you don't know?"
My father's voice would jerk
my little brother from his dream,
and I'd watch him as he plunged
right back again.
"It's ice cream, for Chrissake."

"Vanilla, then."
She'd stab that small,
flat, wooden slice of spoon
into her Dixie cup and churn,
and stare back out her window,
and I'd watch and count
inside my head
(one one-thousand, two one-thousand,
three one-thousand, four . . .)
and wait for her one eye,
half-turned toward me,
for it to blink.
And then I'd hold my breath
and wait again
and she would sigh.

This Is Only a Test (October 1962)

A six-year-old,
I wonder why we crouch so often
under desks at school,
knees drawn to tiny chests,
girls' panties peeking from
beneath our dresses, lace-edged, pink and white.
Checkered floor so cold and clammy,
hiding from—
our teacher never tells us *who,*
but we all know from *what.*
A bomb,
they'll drop a bomb on us
and turn our town to fire,
stop the telephones,
and close the grocery store.
And when that happens,
won't the school fall down on top of us?
I ask our teacher,
looking up while crouched one morning.
"This is just a drill," she answers.
"Keep your head down; no more talking."

That night, I ask my father,
"Won't the school fall down on top of us
when they start dropping bombs?"
He looks up from his newspaper, says, "Who?"
I tell him, "I don't know."
I *want* to tell him,
you and Mom, my little brother,
Murry—he's our dog—
should come to school and hide with me.
He folds the paper.

"You don't know?" He lights himself a Camel as
I shake my head,
he's blowing smoke—
"Then don't worry about it."

Runs with Scissors

You know you could get hurt,
my teacher scolded.
And when she told my mom
who told my dad,
you know I did.

Sit still.
Watch out.
Be careful.
Put that down before you break it.

All that ever broke was me,
a hairline crack
no one could see
unless they got up really close
and that, of course, I learned,
just could not be.

Never let them see you cry,
and don't reveal your secrets.
Be quiet.
No.
Be silent.
And stop that stupid running,
wipe that smirk right off your face.

When I grew tall at last,
I grasped
the silver blades once more,
and did I ever run again,
so very far and very fast,
and never even stumbled.

Today, I swallow shining swords.
On Sundays, I breathe fire.

Dunk

Some fathers teach their children
how to swim,
to ride a bicycle,
to be a better person.
My father taught me how to dunk.

We're at the kitchen table
with the black-and-white
in front of us,
he cuts it so we each get
half the cookie,
each get half the chocolate icing,
half the white.
His coffee cup,
three sugars,
heavy cream,
it lets off steam.
I watch him slowly, carefully
submerge the cookie on the white side,
dunk once more for luck,
then snap it with his teeth.
The chocolate side's a flick-and-switch
so fast that I can hardly see
before he's fishing out the final crumbs
left floating in the cup.

Then it's my turn,
but I can't do it right.

Still Daddy, he's determined
to wrest order out of chaos,
so we practice
till I make him proud,
each mirrored finger movement
worth a smile,
another bite.

Soon I'm a virtuoso,
and we dunk in unison,
swirling crusty bread in homemade gravy
Sundays when the meatballs and spaghetti
are all gone.
Then there's toast in runny, sunny yolks,
and saltines soaked in chicken soup,
egg rolls dipped in mustard hot enough
to melt the metal of the braces on my teeth.

All that time,
I really hated it,
the dripping and the mush, the gloppy mess,
I hate it still.
But Daddy, I loved Daddy,
so I'd sit with him
and gulp
and grin
and after every swallow,
I'd say,
this—
is
really—
good.

Family Barbecue

Grandma's taking out her teeth again.
She's trying to scare the baby,
newest cousin, and
of course, she does.
Her lower jaw is jutting,
choppers chattering,
wrinkles congealing,
face an inch from poor, scared Baby's,
crevices are carving puckered cheeks
and splitting shriveled lips.

Eyes popping, snatching, suddenly,
a daughter's cheap black wig,
the strands of stringy hair
topped by a straw hat, orange bow,
no wonder Baby's squirming,
Baby's shrieking—
I'd be shrieking, too,
except I know my father, Grandma's favorite,
over at the grill—
fat sausage shooting grease across the lawn,
it dots the surface of the backyard, built-in pool,
hamburgers sizzling, draped in yellow cheese—
my father, he would drop his spatula and pointed fork
and chase me, catch me, smack me hard
for disrespecting her, the only woman that he loves.

So I stand still
and go on watching Grandma,
now she's grinning,
Baby hiccupping and gasping,
and its mom, my oldest cousin,
holds on tighter, silent, staring,
as am I
at Grandma,
thinking,
this,
this is the flesh I come from,
this my blood,
those false, ferocious teeth.
I'm thinking of the ones who get to laugh
while all the rest,
they bite their tongues
to keep from screaming.

Grandpa's Weeds

Grandpa's picking weeds again.
My father says, "He's old."
Next week the gardeners will come
and kill those dandelions.
But for today,
it's me and Grandpa,
olive oil,
some pepper, salt, a lemon slice,
a cracked blue bowl,
the greens all slick and shiny,
and we're taking turns,
our fingers dip
and pluck another piece of weed
out of the bowl,
we're slurping,
licking,
laughing, dripping yellow oil
down both our chins,
still laughing,
still we're laughing.
And Daddy, watching,
shakes his head and
lights another Camel,
throws the match
into the kitchen sink
and mutters, "Goddam weeds."

In the Trenches

In the cellar cedar closet,
shut the door
quick
tug the string
that jerks the light on,
single, sizzling bulb,
it's white, it's hot,
I'm crouching
on cold, concrete floor that Grandpa painted
gunshot gray
and breathing in that sharp wood smell
and tracing patterns,
purple-red,
sliced slabs that drip down all the walls,
my cheek against your full-length fur,
the coat so soft and shiny.

Dad said he bought it just for you
before you found a lipstick,
peppermints,
a crumpled tissue in the pocket
and the war broke out again
this time
no terms
no truce.

I think that I could sit here
in this stifled cedar closet,
with no water and no window,
wrapped inside your fur, pretending

I am warm,
not one more casualty,
no reek of death
escaping and
no one would ever notice
that I'm gone.

See You Later, Alligator

Daddy comes to my room and
it's already dark, but I'm not sleeping.
He has to go to work again—
I hear him telling Mom and
she's crying 'cause she misses him
each time he's gone and
so do I.
 But he can't leave until I say,
"See you later, alligator!"
and Daddy kisses my forehead.
"In a while, crocodile," he grins.
"Not too soon, raccoon!" I know the words,
I know my part.
"Don't be—" Daddy winks at me.
"Late!" I shout.
"I won't be," and his fingers brush my cheek—
and then he's gone.

It's our good-luck charm and
we have to say the words the same way
every time and all together—
so Daddy will be safe wherever he goes.

Back beneath my blanket,
I hear the front door close
and Mom still crying,
but I don't get out of bed,
I'm not allowed.

And Daddy has to go to work
a lot of nights,
sometimes even on Sunday.

But he can't leave
until we say our good-luck words,
until he promises he won't be late.

One day he is,
and Mom says it's because
he has another family now.
And that's when I discover
there's a thing called bad luck, too.

Infant of Prague

In second grade my teacher, Mrs. Migdale,
had what grown-ups whispered was a
"nervous breakdown."
Sometimes she'd stand before us,
blackboard at her back,
and sob.
Sometimes she'd yell and curse
and then she'd smile.

When she told us to scissor
schoolwork papers into the shape
of a maple leaf
then staple the pages to make a book
for our parents to look at on Parents' Night,
Caroline Henderson kept cutting
cutting cutting
because her shapes just weren't quite right
until the papers got so small
you couldn't read the spelling words or sums.
Mrs. Migdale really yelled then,
and Caroline was crying.

When Mrs. Migdale stood at my desk,
I could hardly breathe.
I'd look up fast, my eyes afraid,
look into her big nostrils
and I'd hear her bigger voice.

Soon I had stomachaches so bad
I couldn't go to school for days.
But that meant I could curl up in
the big bed my parents still shared.

My mother, quiet anger just as dark
as Mrs. Migdale's,
had to feed me saltine crackers, chicken soup,
Coca-Cola with the bubbles all stirred out.
She'd carry in a tray,
snap, "Now don't bother me, my program's on."
That's when I knew that I would have
an hour with the Infant
on my father's side night table,
painted statue, porcelain, and only
seven inches tall,
robe flowing into frozen folds
of gold and white and lilac
trimmed with pale blue leaves
and dark red blooms,
their centers clear, cut crystal
(I was sure that they were diamonds),
tiny stars and crosses,
then, the golden crown,
the sacred heart a tiny pulse
beneath a frilled glass collar.
Turned upside-down,
the words in perfect, tiny letters read,
"Infant of Prague."
I didn't know where, what Prague was,
I only knew the Infant was so pretty.
And they wouldn't let me touch it
so I touched it all I could.

My father's talisman—
in exchange for its display,
his absolution.

But he didn't take the Infant
when they finally got divorced,
all his sins maybe forgiven
or more likely, all forgotten.
So my mother kept it and I packed it
when she moved to senior living,
set it on a shelf where no one ever looked at it
but me.
And when she died, I packed the Infant up again
and took it to my own house, set it on *my* shelf
with all my other sins arranged.

And now I hold it in my hands
as often as I want to
and in autumn tie a maple leaf
around its infant throat.

September, Starting High School

Every girl remembers her first kiss.

Albert Football Hero slams me
up against hall locker,
metal handle knifes my back,
thick, hairy arms a prison,
wet and wormy tongue
shoved down my throat,
I'm choking
I can't breathe.

Albert doesn't know my name.
It's my first week in high school,
not fourteen yet,
he's a senior,
slicked-back, greasy hair,
black leather and
my favorite dress,
green dotted swiss,
Empire waist,
his hands,
before that afternoon
that dress made me feel pretty.

And no one comes into the hall
to find out why I'm gone so long,
the wooden hall pass
pressed into my throat.
At last he smirks, he lets me go.
I run to general science,
mouth all smeared
and sick,
but no one notices.

I'll never tell.

For days, he follows me,
tongue flicking,
eyebrow raised,
one finger to his puffer-fishy lips
to seal the secret.

Football season
he's so busy with the other
bastard boys
he never stops to watch me now,
not even when we share
a study-hall detention,
and Albert's staring past me
at a silver crucifix that rests
between two bigger breasts.
He licks those lips, he grins,
and turns to me,
my hair a curtain.
"Hey, you got a pencil?"
reaches over, jabs fat finger,
"Hey, I said I need a pencil.
What the hell? You deaf or something, kid?"

I mumble,
"Take it
take it,
what you want,"
run out into the hall,
the teacher hollering,
"Come back here!"

duck into the girls' room,
slam my fist into the mirror,
never tell,
and slam my fist again,
the damn thing still won't shatter.

Mr. Levine Teaches the Goy About Passover

for Myrna

At my best friend's house
to celebrate the Seder,
first night,
special night of grandparents,
uncles, cousins, aunts,
and me,
the one who colors Easter eggs
and loves the smell of
baking ham.

Around the table, Mr. Levine
and the men,
all wearing kippot,
skullcaps, he explains.

I am wearing
my best dress,
color of the purple wine.

Mr. Levine points to the plate.
Parsley dipped in saltwater,
tears of our ancestors.
Lamb shank
roasted egg
sacrifice
sacrifice.
Chopped apple, nuts, and spices,
mortar to build for our masters.

(I Am That I Am,
show kindness.
And if not kindness,
mercy.
And if not mercy,
give us leave to
go our way alone.)
Matzoh, he is saying.
Haste.
Always we flee from
our own demise.
Maror, I am thinking.
Bitter herbs,
I understand.

Bondage.
The uncounted tears and
purple bruises throb to life
like heartbeats
underneath my dress.
Flight.
The promise of
deep water,
Pharaoh cannot follow,

and I know now
why this night is
different,
different from the rest.

Because I am
I am
not there
but here,
in sanctuary.
When he tells of blood
to mark the door,
again,
I understand.

Another Day

My father
would have killed a parakeet
spewing seeds
on the living-room rug,
wringing its blue and yellow body
like a towel in his hands,
his hands,
the right hand,
it was stronger,
grabs my arm above the elbow,
the left hand
smacks across my face,
the fingers each
tattoo my cheek,
my glasses fly
into the wall
and break,
I scoop the pieces,
stumble
to my room
and snatch my books, scotch tape
for when I need to see,
cheese sandwich from the kitchen
where my mother has been busy,
walk out the door
and down the hill,
and he drives past
and doesn't even wave,
and it's another day
that I'll be late for school.

O Holy Night

It's Christmas Eve and we are home alone,
my little brother, me, and the TV.
Our father with his girlfriend and her kids,
our mother just drove off to follow him.

My little brother, me, and the TV.
The Night Before Christmas, Dad used to read to us.
Our mother just drove off to follow him.
I make two cups of cocoa.

The Night Before Christmas, Dad used to read to us.
We trimmed the tree together.
I make two cups of cocoa.
My brother cries, my eyes are dry.

We trimmed the tree together,
but that was long ago.
My brother cries, my eyes are dry,
the stars are brightly shining.

But that was long ago,
and we grew up and still
the stars are brightly shining.
In our hearts we hold that memory.

And we grew up and still,
it's Christmas Eve and we are home alone.
In our hearts, we hold that memory,
our father with his girlfriend and her kids.

High School English Teacher

for Charles T. Tucker, 1936–2016

They laughed at me in class,
the other kids,
because I wrote a poem that rhymed.
I sat far back against the wall
next to a window where
sometimes I'd see a robin
or a weed.

You told them all to stop,
and then you told them all—and me—
the work was good.

I still can hear you shouting,
"Call me Ishmael" and
"Boomlay BOOM,"
warning us against
the measuring with coffee spoons,
reminding us how every word, it matters.

You cracked the nutshell of the world for me.
You were a giant,
you knew everything but fear.
You taught me how to speak
and stand again each time I stumble.

The school year quickly ended,
quickly I became another fading face to you.
Not you to me.
You stayed inside me,
kept me floating even when
I wanted just to swallow salt
and sink into
the sea.

Marriage Material: According to My Father

after Richard Blanco

Don't talk about your job.
(Nobody cares you're a reporter.)
Show him that you can cook—
invite him over for lasagna.
But shave your legs first.
Jesus Christ Almighty, wear a bra.
You want him thinking you're just some *puttana?*

Lose five pounds by Friday.
Only order a Pink Lady.
Let *him* pick the place you go and
let him drive.

Listen to me. I'm your father.
Don't you think you're so damn smart.
How you ever gettin' married like you are?

Ask him about the stuff he does.
Don't quote that goddam Shakespeare.
Tell him his sister's pretty even if the kid's a dog.

Don't end up in the back seat of the car.
You make him wait for it.
You want that ring,
you wanna be the mother of his children,
don't you?
Don't you?

So give him just a taste but no dessert.
Hear what I'm sayin'?
And for Chrissake, don't tell him about the baby.
Or the priest.

Momma

When you die,
what talisman will invoke you,
unleashing all those storm-roiled years?
Here, in your solitary bedroom,
your relic lies
in its scratched and blackened walnut box—
the necklace Daddy gave you,
circular gold disk caught
on coiling golden chain.
One side a devil
forking up a spray of pearls.
Quick flip and switch—
cunning design for cunning play—
the disk reverses to reveal
an angel flashing cut pink stone
held in an upraised hand.

"That's me," you said he told you
when, in reconciliation
short but sweet
before the final split,
he gave you what you cherish still,
three decades after he has gone to dust.
"I'm a devil, but sometimes
I can be an angel, too,"
you said he said
and flashed that grin
he used to melt—
and scorch—
so many hearts.

All those years ago
when you first showed me this,
his final gift,
delighted as a schoolgirl
pinning on her prom corsage,
you didn't know
he'd told me,
filled with pride,
how this charm first had twined
the throat
of his most recent lover,
the one he later married
and the one who watched him die.
Reclaimed after a quarrel,
he turned and offered up her gift
to you,
pretending he'd been thinking
of you only
all along.

Old woman now,
you clasp it close,
recalling—
what?
What might have been?
Sometimes that necklace
gleams on you
and I am blinking sudden tears

for you
for all your legacy,
that twisted,
two-faced chain.

Like Foxfire

They are waiting for her to die.
My aunt in the dark room beside the kitchen
where they argue and shout,
brimming with passion and anger.
If they would whisper truth
even to themselves at night,
they would say

We wish it over
We wish her gone
That hank of hair
That clump of bone
Once sister, once a child.

When she moans in the dark
they yell louder,
enraged at chaos not of their design.
It's a curse, they cry
(as if the dying cannot hear).

I come, bringing daffodils
glowing in the gloom like foxfire,
a word she doesn't understand.
Her only window opens to a brick wall.
Leaning out, peering close,
pinpoint crystals flare from the cement.
I see the sparkle.

Holding the bunch of daffodils
gleaming like foxfire against her skin,
greedily, gratefully, she sinks into the center.
Life flickers from her eyes
as she drinks
I see the sparkle.

My Cousin Angela Keeps It Safe

Now you have the candy dish, lime green,
its handle a chipped-glass, burgundy rose.
Always on the end table when our parents
drove from Jersey to the city, Grandma's,
Thompson Street, each Sunday, homemade
macaroni, gravy (here they call it "sauce"),
meatballs, roasted peppers, crusty bread
from Lafayette Street. Grown-ups
in the kitchen drinking anisette and whiskey,
us out in the living room, pushing each other
off the rocking chair to sit closest
to the candy dish.
Carefully, quietly, one of us would raise
that splintered handle and sneak sour balls
and chocolates.
When they caught us, we got yelled at.
"Can't you wait? It's almost ready."
Sometimes my dad, yours,
would smack us on our butts, not hard.
And then they'd grab a candy, grin, wink,
go back to the kitchen, and we knew
that it was worth it, knew next Sunday
we'd be sneaking treats once more.
I hope you fill that candy dish
with sour balls and chocolates,
put it where the kids will find it
while you're making Sunday dinner,
have a drink for me,
and let them think
they're all getting away with something big.

Seeing the Future/My Father's Eyes

My father is sitting
on the marble-topped table,
legs dangling, swinging
like a child's,
eyes lost in thoughts he cannot share,
his suddenly bald head shining.
He has forgotten the key to his suite
here,
in the hotel
where he treats us
to one last lap of luxury.

Eons earlier
he would have raged at needs denied,
bellowed at the bellboy,
demanding entrance,
denying the fault was his alone.
But now he has called me to open the way.
And when at last I come,
part of me still fearing his fury,
he only stares,
legs pumping rhythmically.
I have it, I tell him. I have the key.
(If only that were true.)
He slides from his seat
with a submission that stuns me
and follows inside.

I never thought I'd wish for wrath,
but now that the light has gone out
on his anger
I want him to shake his fist again.
I want him, I need him, to fight.
I want him to vanquish that flash of the future
so suddenly, fiercely, shining.

Here We Go Again

So a man never woke you
at 4 a.m. just to have sex?

This is a creepy question,
even more so when considering that
the questioner's my mother,
in a restaurant where I am wedged
with her and two old-lady friends,
the waiter pouring water while
Mom pockets sugar packets.
My mother, who so smugly and consistently
reminds me
that she was a virgin
on the night she slid into
the marriage bed.
My mother who,
as usual, is talking of
my father and his selfishness,
his beastly, pre-divorce-court
wants and needs.

How,
how, I ask inside my soul—
the desperation Mom engenders
beading on my forehead—
has she managed to fixate on this,
her favorite theme, once more?
All I said was,
I just bought a new alarm clock.

Thinking About Screaming

Pale sun washes
cold window glass.
Tap tap
wood frame
no curtain
all exposed.
Double-thick and
I can't breathe,
but smooth and wet,
a dog nose-print.
Get down get down.
I scare them all.
Sharp edges
and
a single crack
for where the fist breaks through.

All There Is

cool clear water
and fireflies that vanish
that is all there is . . .
    —Fukuda Chiyo-ni

Here I stand cupping
bits of light
that pour and pulse out
through my skin, between my fingers,
wondering,
how can these creatures,
these,
so small,
be filled with such a certain light
when I am filled with none?

Where I would go
a mirrored gold would rest upon
clear water
that would raise me with
its coolness,
with its stillness.
I would not drink.
I would not breathe.
To vanish would be everything,
enough.

Joker Is Wild

Cigarette butts,
poker game in the trailer on Saturday night,
pigs' knuckles
beer bottles half-empty,
the sour smell drifts to the bedroom.
Sometimes glass breaking
a table turned over,
and I'm thinking, this life that I live,
how I hate it.

A dirge for Coyote
who died with a bullet
punched into his belly
for sniffing the trash at the end of the lot
where his forest begins
with its bird sounds and secrets,
where I want to crawl beneath
wet, crumbled leaves,
fill my mouth with black mud
before somebody else does
and spew it all over the king,
once,
of hearts.

Instead, pack a bag
now it's pink quartz for healing
white feather for wisdom
six spearheads and clubs on
a thin silver chain.
Catch a bus,
open window,
once onto the highway,
pull cards from a deck and
it's fifty-two flutters released to the sky and
who says that you need wings to fly?

Love as Theory

My mother wanted to love me.
I see that now in scrawled
inscriptions in the books
she mailed two thousand miles
to me, where I was safe, I told myself.
(I told myself a lie.)

Poetry, *Black Beauty, Little Women,*
packed in battered boxes
stuffed with her old clothes,
most stained and torn, the buttons gone,
that I was meant to wear because
in some strange sense,
despite the distance,
in her mind,
we two were one.

Beneath the clothes and books,
always a small canned ham,
compressed, congealed, its gristle, fat
encased in gloppy gelatin.
"It's all clear meat!" Mom would enthuse
each time I called to thank her for
her latest offering,
the thought that counts.

What is "clear meat"? I'd ask myself.

Why is my mother so obsessed
with cheap canned ham? I'd wonder.
Why send me rumpled clothes,
write words that now, her life long past,
translate to love
that must have lurked somewhere
inside her crazy, shriveled heart,
that showed itself as scribbles,
rags meant to give warmth,
as pressed, pink pork
sent off to feed the only hunger
she could understand.

After Life

I thought it would be like
getting on a plane,
touching down on puffs of cloud,
fluffed cotton
flushed with purple, saffron, rose,
then the crush, the rush
of getting off,
no false alarms
no flames,
a single slide down the emergency chute,
bouncing on my butt,
a glance at all the other travelers,
grabbing my suitcase
then on my way.

But this death thing
is fun-house mirrors stretching my jaw
into my knees,
skeleton teeth gaunt, gleaming.
Candy apples
tilt-a-whirl
carousel
won't let me off
a sudden blast of wind but still
I wait to meet with God
and ride the roller coaster side by side.
Instead, I'm blown across the boardwalk
to Madame Marie's,
her Psychic Booth,
Temple of Knowledge,
back again in Asbury Park
where I already came from once,
where she will read my future,
take me for another ride.

Home Is Where You Hang Your Hat

My uncle used to tell me,
home
is where you hang your hat,
and I'd think,
if you only knew
the places I've hung mine—
in the back of a puke-green Volkswagen van
(but then again, who hasn't?),
on a playground slide
(don't even ask),
one midnight on a beach
in the Bahamas
with some guy named Mike,
those waves kept rising, pounding—
till the sand fleas
wrecked the mood.
In my boyfriend's dorm,
a mattress on the floor,
his roommate's mother
on a Sunday, early, suddenly
she's standing there.
(Why Izzy gave his mom a key,
he never could explain.)
And she's glaring down at us,
her nostrils flaring,
boyfriend snoring,
me flat on my back, buck naked,
but I always was polite.
"Oh good morning, Mrs. Dubin,"
I can still remember saying.

Now much older, slightly wiser,
I don't hang my hat as often.
When I do, it's in a king-size
with room service, penthouse view.
And I always tip quite well;
I'm still polite.

It Could Have Gone Another Way

At college when my dad says
he'll drive down
and take me out to dinner,
and I'm so glad
he wants to spend some time with me alone.
Instead,
he brings his mistress
and her monster Afghan hound
that looks a lot like her.
At least I don't tell her so.
At least my mother never knows about this.

First vacation on my own
with just my girlfriends,
Truro beach where
I meet Norm from Canada.
We go to his hotel, my girlfriends
don't know where I am.
And then I change my mind,
Norm and his friend, they
could have raped me, killed me.
Instead, we fall asleep.
Next morning, we eat scrambled eggs and toast,
Norm drives me back.

Ginger's puppy, Trouble,
falls into the cellar sump pit, left uncovered,
I hear noises Sunday morning,
no one else wakes up,
and I'm just eight, I follow strange sounds
down the stairs, there's Trouble standing,
front paws scratching, scraping, water to his neck,

he's whining, can't get out, he's cold, he's scared,
I pull him up, all soaked and shivering,
and get a rag and pat him dry
and hold him on my lap until he falls asleep.

A stranger's car is rolling
down the Post Office parking lot,
the driver's door unlocked, the car moves
slow enough for me to grab the door handle,
open the door, jump in, stomp on the brake,
pull up on the emergency.
It doesn't hit the brick wall,
roll out on the sidewalk or the street.
Instead, I get the car to stop,
sit,
waiting,
for its owner.

It's amazing, I mean it.
That I have survived.
That I could save someone, myself,
could save *something*.

But I offer my spirit as proof of these things.
How it wakes
a little more each day.
Speaking and standing
and no longer frightened.
Looking into eyes.
Trying again.
Grinning.

Even with the missing tooth.

About the Author

Lynda La Rocca is a New York City-born poet and freelance writer who has also worked as a teaching assistant and a municipal and general-assignment reporter for New Jersey's *Asbury Park Press.*

Lynda's four previous poetry-chapbook collections include *Spiral* (Liquid Light Press, 2012) and *Unbroken* (Kelsay Books, 2023). Her individual poems have appeared in such publications as *Frogpond* (Haiku Society of America), *The New York Quarterly, The Wall Street Journal, The Colorado Sun,* and *Light, a journal of light verse since 1992.*

She was the first-place winner in the poetry category of the 2020 Soul-Making Keats Literary Competition, an arts outreach program of the National League of American Pen Women, and a "Top-Four" winner in the 2021 Maria W. Faust Sonnet Contest.

Lynda has taught adult-education poetry, presented poetry workshops at numerous venues, and served as a judge in dozens of state, national, and international poetry contests. She loves writing, reading, cooking (and eating), learning about wine, watching figure skating, hiking, birding, spending lots of time in nature, and performing her poetry solo and as a member of the River City Nomads' performance-poetry troupe. Lynda lives in Salida, Colorado, with her writer-photographer husband Steve Voynick.

www.ingramcontent.com/pod-product-compliance
Lightning Source LLC
Chambersburg PA
CBHW031205160426
43193CB00008B/516